Table of Contents

Introduction 4

How to Use This Book 5

Learning 1oo Sight Words, Step by Step! 5

A Lesson Plan for Teaching 1oo Sight Words 5

Using the Mini-Books 6

Using the Review, Write, Remember! Sheet 7

Using Fabulous Fill-ins 8

Using the Sight-Word Bingo Game 8

Using Word-Search Puzzles 9

Using the Fun Flash Cards 9

Using Read & Spell Flash Cards for Quick Evaluations 11

Using Read & Spell Flash Cards to Build Skills at Home 11

Formal Assessments 12

Using the Strategic Assessment Tool 12

Evaluating Sight-Word Spelling 12

Reproducibles

1o Make & Share Stories: Mini-Books 15

Fabulous Fill-ins: Using Words in Context 35

Review, Write, Remember!: Practice Pages 45

Sight-Word Bingo Cards: Game Boards 46

Word-Search Puzzles 67

Fun Flash Cards! 77

Strategic Assessment Tool 88

Take-Home Note to Families 89

Read & Spell Flash Cards 9o

Celebrate Achievement 91

Certificate of Achievement 92

Word-Search Answer Key 93

Introduction

Welcome to *Learning Sight Words Is Easy!* As you know, students encounter sight words in the print of their favorite literature, street signs, cereal boxes, and most everywhere. From my own classroom experience, I've found that when emergent readers can readily recall sight words, they become better, more fluent readers. I know that teaching basic sight, or high-frequency, words makes that reading success happen. For that reason, I've shared effective activities that make the process of teaching sight words more manageable and the learning of sight words more enjoyable for kids. I think you'll find teaching and learning 100 sight words has never been easier or more fun!

when

said

will

is

that

was

they

but

an

their

we

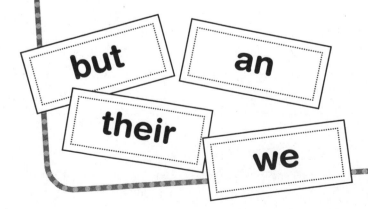

How to Use This Book

Learning 100 Sight Words, Step by Step!

Use the grid below to locate specific words covered in this book. Please note that in order to make instruction more manageable, the 100 sight words have been divided into ten groups of ten. As you plan lessons, you may find the Suggested Sequence for Teaching on page 6 particularly helpful.

Words	Sight Words
1-10	the, of, and, a, to, in, is, you, that, it
11-20	he, for, was, on, are, as, with, his, they, at
21-30	be, this, from, I, have, or, by, one, had, not
31-40	but, what, all, were, when, we, there, can, an, your
41-50	which, their, said, if, do, will, each, about, how, up
51-60	out, them, then, she, many, some, so, these, would, other
61-70	into, has, more, her, two, like, him, see, time, could
71-80	no, make, than, first, been, its, who, now, people, my
81-90	made, over, did, down, only, way, find, use, may, water
91-100	long, little, very, after, words, called, just, where, most, know

A Lesson Plan for Teaching 100 Sight Words

The sequence on page 6 has been provided to help you develop lesson plans. For each group of ten sight words, you'll find a mini-book and several companion activities. Begin teaching each set of ten sight words by reading the mini-book aloud; this will help students learn sight words within the context of a story. After you have read the mini-book, use the flexible companion activities to practice and reinforce sight-word learning. Of course, you should always feel free to develop alternate sequences for teaching to meet your specific needs.

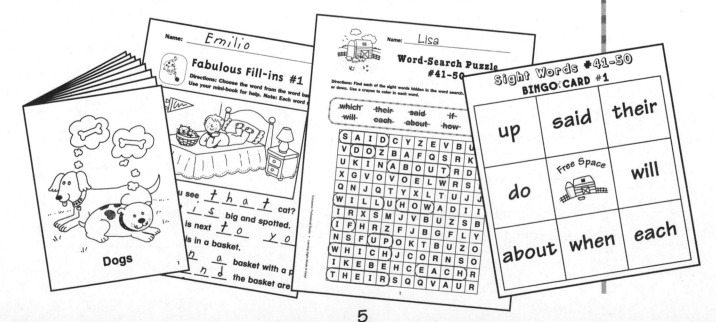

Teacher Tip!

Suggested Sequence for Teaching Each Set of Ten Words

- Mini-Book
- Fabulous Fill-ins
- Review, Write, Remember! Sheet
- Fun Flash Cards
- Sight-Word Bingo
- Word-Search Puzzle
- A Quick Evaluation: Read & Spell Flash Cards and the Take-Home Note to Families

What follows are easy how-to's for making each of these fun-filled activities work for your students.

Using the Mini-Books

Mini-books are a great way to introduce kids to sight words. Work with the class as a whole, engaging children in a discussion about the story.

Dogs

- Show them the cover. Then ask your students to predict what might happen in the story.
- Read the mini-book aloud.
- Revisit each of the ten sight words that appear in the story.
- Encourage children to read through their mini-books on their own, building key reading strategies.
- Remember that mini-books may be used for shared reading and independent reading.

He is with his friend.

They are looking for a bone.

How to Make the Mini-Books:

- Cut along the dotted lines of the mini-book.

- Sequence pages by number.

- Staple the left edge of the pages, securing them in a typical book format.

- Invite kids to color the pictures in their books.

Teacher Tip!

Celebrate developing reading skills by storing mini-books in a place easily accessible to kids, a sort of mini-book library. Reading mini-books on a daily basis will help children build fluency and confidence as readers.

Mini-Book Library

Using the Review, Write, Remember! Sheet

Use the Review, Write, Remember! Sheet on page 45 to reinforce correct spelling and usage of sight words.

- Begin by asking students to reread the sight words within the corresponding mini-book, reviewing sight words within the context of a story.

- Then invite students to write the word list down the left side of their Review, Write, Remember! Sheet.

- Encourage your students to say each sight word quietly to themselves, linking their oral vocabulary with sight-word learning and stimulating memory.

Date: 5-2-00

Name: Cecily

Review, Write, Remember!

Sight Words 81 through 90

Reread the matching storybook, reviewing the spelling and usage of the ten sight words you are currently studying.
Write the word list once down the left side of the page.
Reread each word to check spelling.
Check his/her work.

made
over
did
down
only
way
find
use
may
water

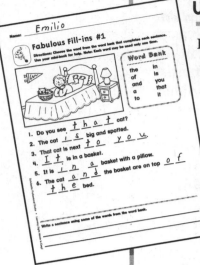

Using Fabulous Fill-ins

Help kids use sight words in the context of sentences with the Fabulous Fill-in reproducibles on pages 35–44. Some students may find it helpful to refer to the mini-book as they work, using the language of the mini-book as a guide.

- Invite students to use sight words to complete the appropriate Fabulous Fill-in, working in small groups, pairs, or independently.

- If you like, ask children to exchange papers to correct one another's work.

Using the Sight-Word Bingo Game

The reproducible Fun Flash Cards on pages 77–87 make great cue cards for Sight-Word Bingo. During play, students draw from the Fun Flash Cards deck and search for the matching sight word on their game board.

- Provide copies of the Fun Flash Cards and reproducible boards on pages 46–66 for your students.
- Supply children with game pieces such as buttons, dried beans, or Bingo chips.

Playing Bingo: Invite students to play Bingo at their desks singly, in pairs, small groups, or as a whole class. On pages 46 through 66 you'll find Bingo game boards for up to eight children to play cooperatively, with one winner. If more than eight children are involved in play, please be aware that there will be more than one winner. If you like, lessen the element of competition—Make a rule that the class hasn't collectively "won" until everyone has declared "Bingo!"

- To play, children will need to set up the game boards, game pieces, and Fun Flash Cards on a desktop or table. To begin the game, the "caller" picks a card from the flash card deck and turns it faceup. Then, he or she reads the word aloud to the other players.

- The "players" search their individual Bingo boards for the matching sight word. If there is a match, they need to place a game piece on the word.

- Encourage your students to continue the process until each of them reaches Bingo. Bingo is achieved when a vertical or horizontal row is completely covered with game pieces. If the players do not reach Bingo, then they need to reshuffle the flash cards, turn them facedown, and continue playing.

Teacher Tip!

Invite more advanced readers to participate with two or more Bingo game cards as an extra challenge.

Using the Word-Search Puzzles

The Word-Search Puzzles in this book will help build fluency by enabling kids to isolate sight words within text. You'll find the reproducible Word-Search Puzzles on pages 67–76 and the answer key on page 93.

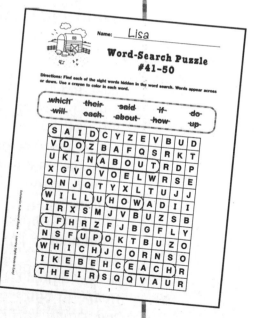

- Discuss the ways in which words may appear in the puzzle—vertically and horizontally.

- Remind your students that there are ten sight words in each puzzle and no sight word appears more than once.

Using the Fun Flash Cards

The reproducible Fun Flash Cards on pages 77–87 can be used as traditional flash cards or for playing Sight Word Bingo, concentration, and more. If you like, place a few decks of laminated Fun Flash Cards in your language arts center. You may even find that their compact size makes them a perfect fit in pocket charts! However you plan to use them, you're sure to discover how Fun Flash Cards make teaching sight words easier.

Playing Concentration: First, copy two sets of the flash cards for several groups of three to four students. You may find it helpful to determine the small groups ahead of time, making the transition to groups faster and easier.

- Ask students to shuffle the flash cards and lay them on the table face-down in rows.
- Remind children to take turns turning over two cards at a time, looking for two words that match. When a student finds two words that match, he or she may take another turn.
- Invite kids to continue playing until every Fun Flash Card has been matched and removed from play.

Teacher Tips!

- Developing stories from Fun Flash Cards is a great way to put student reading skills into action. Invite your students to use flash cards as a word bank for story writing.

- Ask your students to read one Fun Flash Card as a "ticket" to go home at the end of the school day. Later in the school year, have each student spell a word orally before being dismissed from the classroom.

Using Read & Spell Flash Cards for Quick Evaluations

Use the Read & Spell Flash Cards reproducible on page 90 to learn how well your students are learning sight words. For one-on-one evaluations with your students, write the sight words your class is studying on a blank copy of the reproducible page. Then make copies for each member of the class and a copy for yourself. You'll need to cut your copy of the reproducible into flash cards. Now you're ready to evaluate your students. Find a quiet spot and invite a student to join you.

- Place one of your flash cards on the table and ask the student to identify the word.

- Flip the flash card over, facedown. Ask him or her to spell the sight word either orally or write it on a separate piece of paper.

- Note on the Read & Spell Flash Card sheet whether the child needs to focus on spelling or reading the sight word. Circle *R* on the flash card if the child needs to learn how to *read* the word. Circle *S* if the child needs to learn how to *spell* the word.

- After you have evaluated each of your students, make copies for your records. If you like, send one copy home with the Take-Home Note to Families so that parents can reinforce learning at home.

Using Read & Spell Flash Cards to Build Skills at Home

Since flash cards help students direct their focus on one word at a time, they're a terrific way to reinforce sight-word learning. Plus, the Read & Spell Flash Cards are easy to make and great for homework! Just have students follow the directions on the top of the Read & Spell Flash Cards reproducible on page 90. Then your students can toss the flash cards in a bag and practice reading most anywhere, including bus rides, plane trips, vacations—even the living room sofa!

Formal Assessments

A few times a year, it's a good idea to perform formal assessments. (Three to four times a year works well for most teachers.) You're sure to find a routine that fits comfortably with your literacy program.

Using the Strategic Assessment Tool

To help determine how well your students are able to read sight words, use the Strategic Assessment Tool reproducible on page 88. Find a quiet place in the classroom where you can meet with students individually.

- Hold an index card under each word on the Strategic Assessment Tool. The index card helps to isolate the word on the page, making the task of identifying the sight word easier.

- Ask each student to identify the sight word. Check off each word that he or she reads correctly on the Strategic Assessment Tool.

Evaluating Sight-Word Spelling

Evaluating each student's ability to spell sight words provides you with valuable insight. If you like, assess spelling as a whole-class activity.

- Begin the process by providing each student with a piece of lined paper.
- Inform your students that you will be reading each sight word aloud twice, pausing for few moments between readings.
- Ask them to write the correct spelling of each sight word on their paper.
- After you have read the entire selected list of sight words, invite your students to look over their spelling.
- Evaluate your students' work.

Just Getting Started?

A scertaining which words children know when they arrive in September or establishing the base line at the start of the school year is essential. When you have a base line assessment, you provide yourself with a point of reference. You then have a way of evaluating which sight words each child has learned.

Celebrate!: Use the reproducible Certificate of Achievement on page 92 to show your enthusiasm for student learning. Kids love to celebrate success.

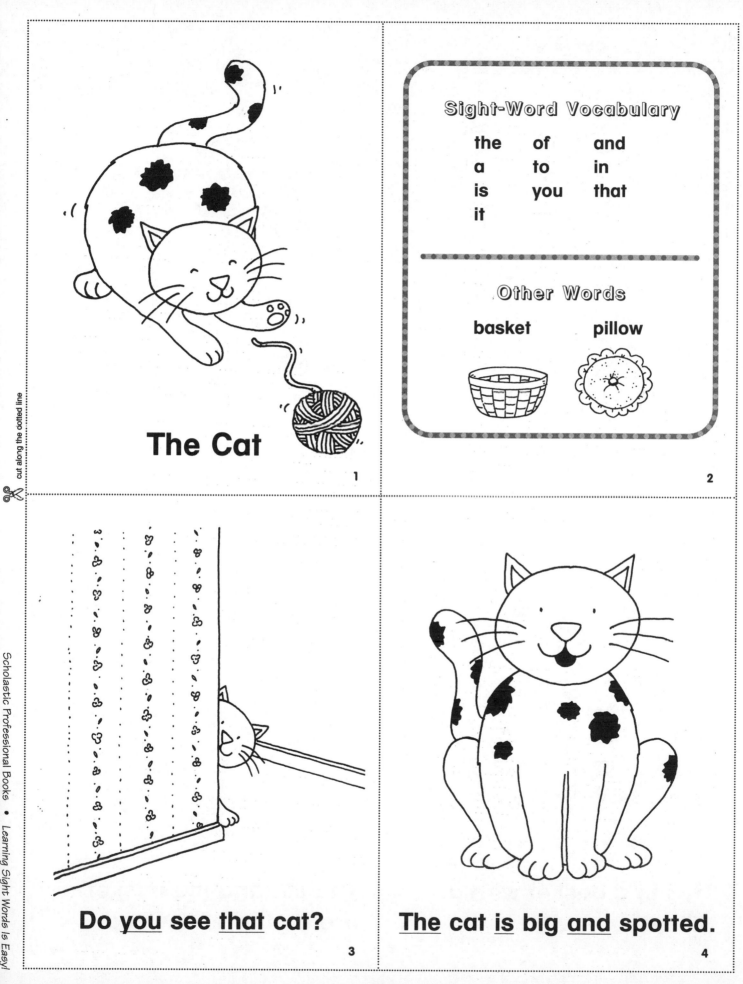

The Cat

1

Sight-Word Vocabulary

the   of   and
a   to   in
is   you   that
it

Other Words

basket   pillow

2

Do <u>you</u> see <u>that</u> cat?

3

<u>The</u> cat <u>is</u> big <u>and</u> spotted.

4

That cat is next to you.

5

It is in a basket.

6

**It is in a basket with a
pillow.**

7

**The cat and the basket
are on top of the bed.**

8

16

Scholastic Professional Books • Learning Sight Words Is Easy!

Dogs

1

Sight-Word Vocabulary

he	for	was
on	are	as
with	his	they
at		

Other Words

bone   tree   grass

2

This is Fred. <u>He</u> is a dog.

3

Fred is <u>as</u> white <u>as</u> snow.

4

17

He is **with** **his** friend.

5

They **are** looking **for** a bone.

6

They look **at** the tree and **on** the grass.

7

They do not see the bone. It **was** gone.

8

Scholastic Professional Books ● Learning Sight Words Is Easy!

The Bird

1

Sight-Word Vocabulary

be	this	from
I	have	or
by	one	had
not		

Other Words

cage   bird

2

I had one bird. His name was Sam.

3

That is why I have this cage.

4

Sam <u>had</u> <u>this</u> cage.

5

He <u>had</u> come <u>from</u> the pet store.

6

Sam could <u>not</u> sing <u>or</u> talk.

7

He just liked to <u>be</u> <u>by</u> me.

8

cut along the dotted line

The Beach

1

Sight-Word Vocabulary

but	what	all
were	when	we
there	can	an
your		

Other Words

beach   fish

octopus   whale

shark   starfish

<u>We</u> <u>were</u> at the beach.

3

<u>All</u> of the fish <u>were</u> <u>there</u>.

4

21

We saw **an** octopus **but** not a whale.

5

We even saw a shark.

6

We saw **your** favorite, a starfish!

7

What can you see **when** you go to the beach?

8

Scholastic Professional Books • *Learning Sight Words Is Easy!*

A Farm

1

Sight-Word Vocabulary

which	their	said
if	do	will
each	about	how
up		

Other Words

farm	book	road

2

Each of us knows **how** to read a book **about** a farm.

3

"**Which** book **will** we read today?" **said** Ann.

4

"**<u>Do</u>** you like this book?"
<u>said</u> Ben.
　"Yes," **<u>said</u>** Ann.

5

Ann and Ben read **<u>their</u>**
book.

6

"I would like to see a cow,
<u>if</u> we can," **<u>said</u>** Ben.

7

"There is a farm **<u>up</u>** the
road," **<u>said</u>** Ann.

8

Dolls

1

Sight-Word Vocabulary

out	them	then
she	many	some
so	these	would
other		

Other Words

dolls

2

Sue had <u>many</u> dolls, like <u>these.</u>

3

<u>Some</u> of <u>them</u> were big.

4

25

Other dolls were small.

5

Sue would take her big dolls **out**.

6

Then she would play with **them**.

7

Sue had **so** much fun with her dolls!

8

Scholastic Professional Books • *Learning Sight Words Is Easy!*

The Watch

1

Sight-Word Vocabulary

into	has	more
her	two	like
him	see	time
could		

Other Words

watch   car   box

2

Did you <u>see</u> the watch
Jack put <u>into</u> a box?

3

His watch looks <u>like</u> a car.

4

It <u>has</u> <u>two</u> hands, wheels, and <u>more</u>.

5

It even tells the <u>time</u> to <u>him</u>.

6

Maria would <u>like</u> a watch <u>like</u> a car.

7

Jack <u>could</u> give it to <u>her</u>!

8

tic toc tic toc
It is now
three
o'clock

Scholastic Professional Books • Learning Sight Words Is Easy!

cut along the dotted line

The Bike

1

Sight-Word Vocabulary

no	make	than
first	been	its
who	now	people
my		

Other Words

bike   wheels   sad

2

I have <u>been</u> sad with <u>no</u> bike.

3

<u>Who</u> can <u>make</u> <u>my</u> bike with me?

4

First, put on **its** two wheels.

5

Now put on the seat.

6

I can ride better **than** before.

7

I will show the **people** what I can do **now**.

8

Scholastic Professional Books • *Learning Sight Words Is Easy!*

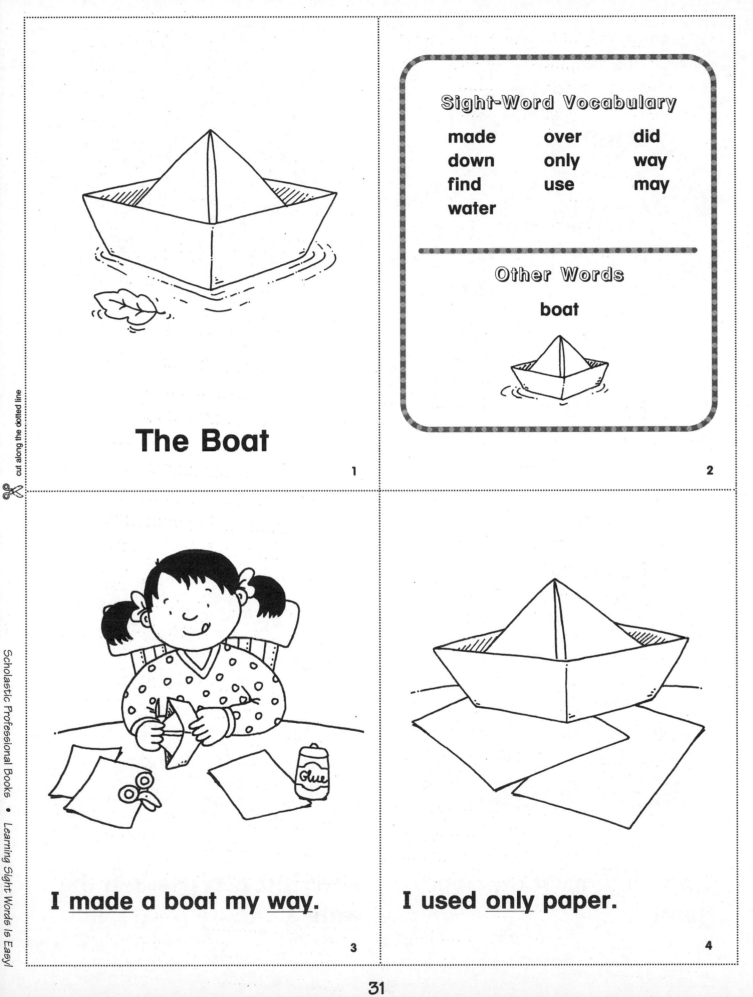

cut along the dotted line

The Boat

1

Sight-Word Vocabulary

made	over	did
down	only	way
find	use	may
water		

Other Words

boat

2

I <u>made</u> a boat my <u>way</u>.

3

I used <u>only</u> paper.

4

May I go **down** to the water?

5

The **water** is **over** there.

6

I will **find** out if my boat floats.

7

I **did** it! I can **use** it in the **water!**

8

Scholastic Professional Books • *Learning Sight Words Is Easy!*

long just
called words
where after
little know
very most

Words

1

2

just

very

Do you <u>know</u> how to read these <u>words</u>?

3

little

words

<u>Most</u> of them are <u>little</u> words.

4

just
very
long

Just a very few are long words.

5

after

"After" is an easy word to read.

6

called
where

"Called" and "where" are hard words to read.

7

long   just
called   words
where   after
little   know
very   most

Did you read all of these words?

8

Scholastic Professional Books • *Learning Sight Words Is Easy!*

Fabulous Fill-ins #1

Directions: Choose the word from the word bank that completes each sentence. Use your mini-book for help. Note: Each word may be used only one time.

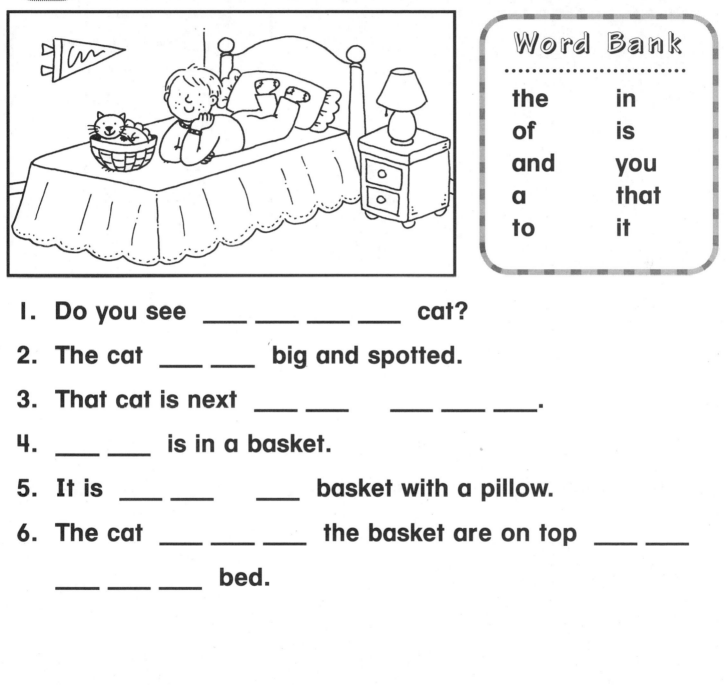

Word Bank

the	in
of	is
and	you
a	that
to	it

1. Do you see ___ ___ ___ ___ cat?

2. The cat ___ ___ big and spotted.

3. That cat is next ___ ___   ___ ___ ___.

4. ___ ___ is in a basket.

5. It is ___ ___   ___ basket with a pillow.

6. The cat ___ ___ ___ the basket are on top ___ ___ ___ ___ ___ bed.

Write a sentence using some of the words from the word bank.

_____

_____

Fabulous Fill-ins #2

Directions: Choose the word from the word bank that completes each sentence. Use your mini-book for help. Note: Each word may be used only one time.

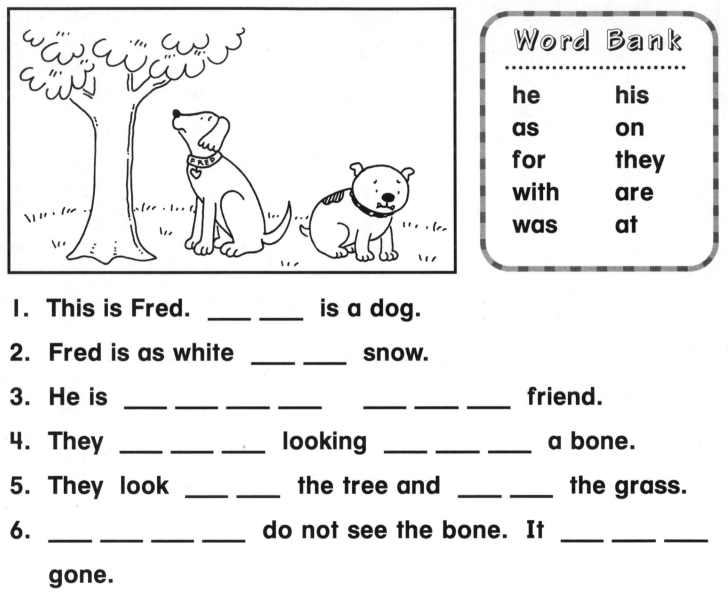

Word Bank

he	his
as	on
for	they
with	are
was	at

1. This is Fred. ___ ___ is a dog.

2. Fred is as white ___ ___ snow.

3. He is ___ ___ ___ ___   ___ ___ ___ friend.

4. They ___ ___ ___ looking ___ ___ ___ a bone.

5. They look ___ ___ the tree and ___ ___ the grass.

6. ___ ___ ___ ___ do not see the bone. It ___ ___ ___ gone.

Write a sentence using some of the words from the word bank.

_____

_____

Scholastic Professional Books • *Learning Sight Words Is Easy!*

Fabulous Fill-ins #3

Directions: Choose the word from the word bank that completes each sentence. Use your mini-book for help. Note: Each word may be used only one time.

Word Bank

be	or
this	by
from	one
I	had
have	not

1. ___ had ___ ___ ___ bird. His name was Sam.

2. That is why I ___ ___ ___ ___ ___ ___ ___ ___ cage.

2. Sam ___ ___ ___ this cage.

4. He had come ___ ___ ___ ___ the pet store.

5. Sam could ___ ___ ___ sing ___ ___ talk.

6. He just liked to ___ ___ ___ ___ me.

Write a sentence using some of the words from the word bank.

_____

_____

Scholastic Professional Books • Learning Sight Words Is Easy!

Fabulous Fill-ins #4

Directions: Choose the word from the word bank that completes each sentence. Use your mini-book for help. Note: Each word may be used only one time.

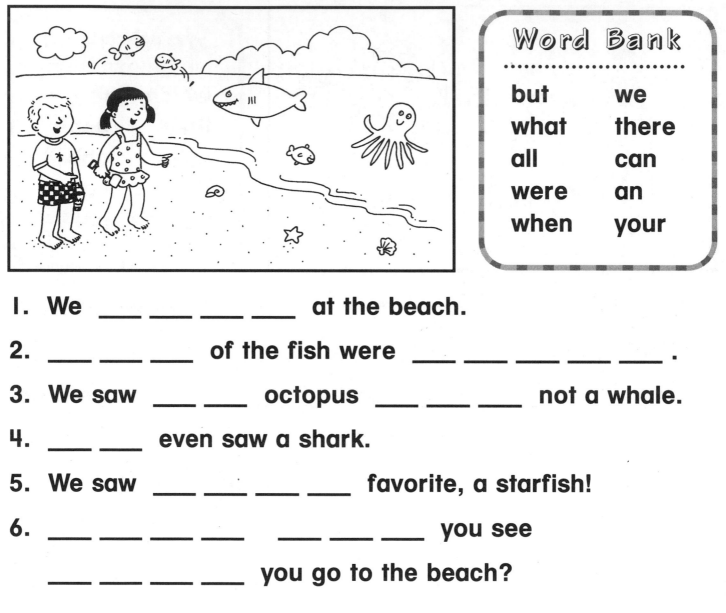

Word Bank

but	we
what	there
all	can
were	an
when	your

1. We ___ ___ ___ ___ at the beach.

2. ___ ___ ___ of the fish were ___ ___ ___ ___ ___ .

3. We saw ___ ___ octopus ___ ___ ___ not a whale.

4. ___ ___ even saw a shark.

5. We saw ___ ___ ___ ___ favorite, a starfish!

6. ___ ___ ___ ___ ___ ___ ___ ___ you see

___ ___ ___ ___ you go to the beach?

Write a sentence using some of the words from the word bank.

_____

_____

Scholastic Professional Books • *Learning Sight Words Is Easy!*

Fabulous Fill-ins #5

Directions: Choose the word from the word bank that completes each sentence. Use your mini-book for help. Note: Each word may be used only one time.

Word Bank

which	will
their	each
said	about
if	how
do	up

1. ___ __ __ ___ of us knows ___ ___ ___ to read a book ___ __ __ __ ___ a farm .

2. "__ __ __ __ __ book ___ __ __ ___ we read today?" said Ann.

3. "___ ___ you like this book?" said Ben. "Yes," ___ __ __ ___ Ann.

4. Ann and Ben read ___ __ __ __ __ book.

5. "I would like to see a cow, ___ ___ we can," said Ben.

6. "There is a farm ___ ___ the road," said Ann.

Write a sentence using some of the words from the word bank.

_____

_____

Scholastic Professional Books • Learning Sight Words Is Easy!

Fabulous Fill-ins #6

Directions: Choose the word from the word bank that completes each sentence. Use your mini-book for help. Note: Each word may be used only one time.

Word Bank

out	some
them	so
then	these
she	would
many	other

1. Sue had ___ ___ ___ ___ dolls, like

   ___ ___ ___ ___ ___ .

2. ___ ___ ___ ___ of them were big.

3. ___ ___ ___ ___ dolls were small.

4. Sue ___ ___ ___ ___ ___ take her big dolls

   ___ ___ ___ .

5. ___ ___ ___ ___ ___ ___ ___ ___ would play with

   ___ ___ ___ ___ .

6. Sue had ___ ___ much fun with her dolls!

Write a sentence using some of the words from the word bank.

_____

_____

Fabulous Fill-ins #7

Directions: Choose the word from the word bank that completes each sentence.
Use your mini-book for help. Note: Each word may be used only one time.

Word Bank

into	like
has	him
more	see
her	time
two	could

1. Did you ___ ___ ___ the watch Jack put ___ ___ ___ ___ a box?

2. His watch looks ___ ___ ___ ___ like a car than a watch.

3. It ___ ___ ___   ___ ___ ___ hands, wheels, and more.

4. It even tells the ___ ___ ___ ___ to ___ ___ ___ .

5. Maria would ___ ___ ___ ___ a watch like a car.

6. Jack ___ ___ ___ ___ ___ give it to ___ ___ ___ !

Write a sentence using some of the words from the word bank.

_____

_____

Fabulous Fill-ins #8

Directions: Choose the word from the word bank that completes each sentence. Use your mini-book for help. Note: Each word may be used only one time.

Word Bank

no	its
make	who
than	now
first	people
been	my

1. I have ___ ___ ___ ___ sad with ___ ___ bike.

2. ___ ___ ___ can ___ ___ ___ ___ ___ ___ bike with me?

3. ___ ___ ___ ___ ___ , put on ___ ___ ___ two wheels.

4. ___ ___ ___ put on the seat.

5. I can ride better ___ ___ ___ ___ before.

6. I will show the ___ ___ ___ ___ ___ ___ what I can do now.

Write a sentence using some of the words from the word bank.

_____

_____

Scholastic Professional Books • Learning Sight Words Is Easy!

Name: _____

Fabulous Fill-ins #9

Directions: Choose the word from the word bank that completes each sentence. Use your mini-book for help. Note: Each word may be used only one time.

Word Bank

made	way
over	find
did	use
down	may
only	water

1. I ___ ___ ___ ___ a boat my ___ ___ ___ .

2. I used ___ ___ ___ ___ paper.

3. ___ ___ ___ I go ___ ___ ___ ___ to the water?

4. The ___ ___ ___ ___ ___ is ___ ___ ___ ___ there.

5. I will ___ ___ ___ ___ out if my boat floats.

6. I ___ ___ ___ it! I can ___ ___ ___ it in the water!

Write a sentence using some of the words from the word bank.

_____

_____

Fabulous Fill-ins #10

Directions: Choose the word from the word bank that completes each sentence. Use your mini-book for help. Note: Each word may be used only one time.

long   just   called
words   where
little   know   most
very   after

Word Bank
....

long	called
little	just
very	where
after	most
words	know

1. Do you ___ ___ ___ ___ how to read these words?

2. ___ ___ ___ ___ of them are ___ ___ ___ ___ ___ ___ words.

3. ___ ___ ___ ___ a ___ ___ ___ ___ few are ___ ___ ___ ___ words.

4. " ___ ___ ___ ___ ___ " is an easy word to read.

5. " ___ ___ ___ ___ ___ ___ " and " ___ ___ ___ ___ ___ " are hard words to read.

4. Did you read all of these ___ ___ ___ ___ ___ ?

Write a sentence using some of the words from the word bank.

_____

_____

Scholastic Professional Books • *Learning Sight Words Is Easy!*

Review, Write, Remember!

Sight Words

_____ through _____ .

Reread the matching storybook, reviewing the spelling and usage of the ten sight words you are currently studying.

Write the word list once down the left side of the page.

Reread each word to check spelling.

Check your work.

Sight-Word Bingo Cards #1-10

Directions: Reproduce, laminate, and cut each card.

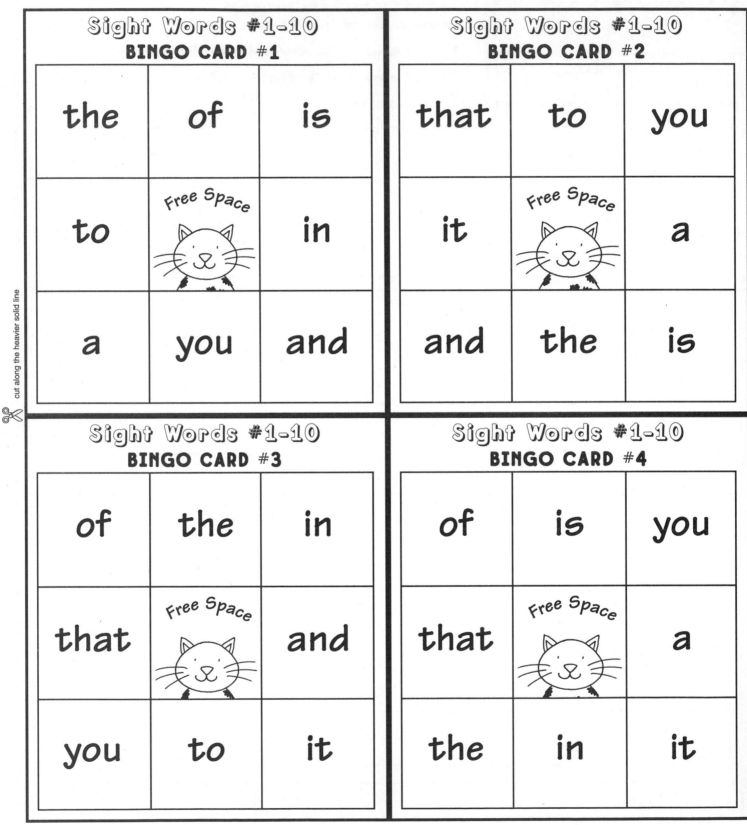

Sight Words #1-10
BINGO CARD #1

the	of	is
to	Free Space	in
a	you	and

Sight Words #1-10
BINGO CARD #2

that	to	you
it	Free Space	a
and	the	is

Sight Words #1-10
BINGO CARD #3

of	the	in
that	Free Space	and
you	to	it

Sight Words #1-10
BINGO CARD #4

of	is	you
that	Free Space	a
the	in	it

Sight-Word Bingo Cards #1-10

Directions: Reproduce, laminate, and cut each card.

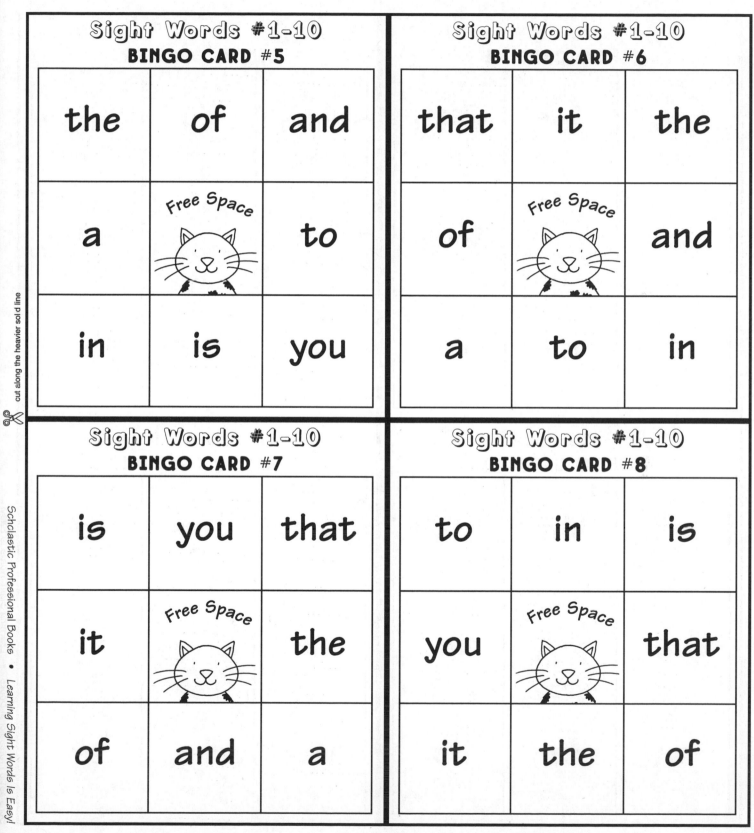

Sight Words #1-10
BINGO CARD #5

the	of	and
a	Free Space	to
in	is	you

Sight Words #1-10
BINGO CARD #6

that	it	the
of	Free Space	and
a	to	in

Sight Words #1-10
BINGO CARD #7

is	you	that
it	Free Space	the
of	and	a

Sight Words #1-10
BINGO CARD #8

to	in	is
you	Free Space	that
it	the	of

cut along the heavier solid line

Scholastic Professional Books • Learning Sight Words Is Easy!

47

Sight-Word Bingo Cards #11-20

Directions: Reproduce, laminate, and cut each card.

cut along the heavier solid line

Sight Words #11-20
BINGO CARD #1

at	for	with
as	Free Space	they
on	he	was

Sight Words #11-20
BINGO CARD #2

with	for	his
as	Free Space	was
on	are	they

Sight Words #11-20
BINGO CARD #3

are	he	with
was	Free Space	at
on	for	his

Sight Words #11-20
BINGO CARD #4

they	are	was
as	Free Space	his
with	he	at

Sight-Word Bingo Cards #11-20

Directions: Reproduce, laminate, and cut each card.

Sight Words #11-20
BINGO CARD #5

he	for	was
on	Free Space FRED	are
as	with	his

Sight Words #11-20
BINGO CARD #6

they	at	he
for	Free Space FRED	was
on	are	as

Sight Words #11-20
BINGO CARD #7

with	his	they
at	Free Space FRED	he
for	was	on

Sight Words #11-20
BINGO CARD #8

are	as	with
his	Free Space FRED	they
at	he	for

Sight-Word Bingo Cards #21-30

Directions: Reproduce, laminate, and cut each card.

Sight Words #21-30
BINGO CARD #1

from	had	be
one	*Free Space*	or
by	this	not

Sight Words #21-30
BINGO CARD #2

one	from	or
have	*Free Space*	had
this	I	not

Sight Words #21-30
BINGO CARD #3

be	by	from
I	*Free Space*	had
have	not	this

Sight Words #21-30
BINGO CARD #4

be	had	I
from	*Free Space*	by
have	this	one

Scholastic Professional Books • *Learning Sight Words Is Easy!*

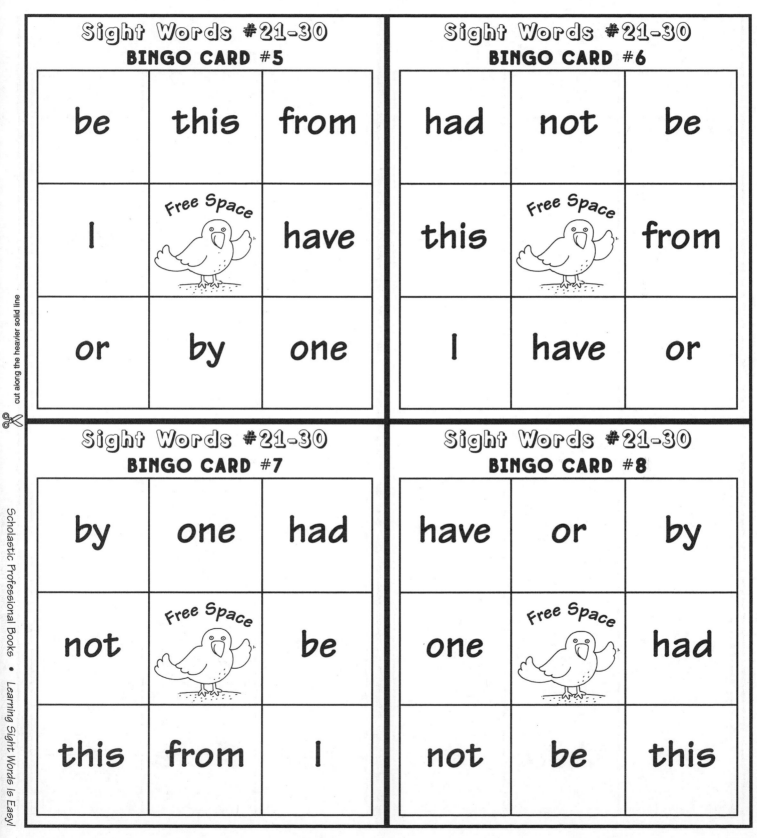

Sight Words #21-30
BINGO CARD #5

be	this	from
I	Free Space	have
or	by	one

Sight Words #21-30
BINGO CARD #6

had	not	be
this	Free Space	from
I	have	or

Sight Words #21-30
BINGO CARD #7

by	one	had
not	Free Space	be
this	from	I

Sight Words #21-30
BINGO CARD #8

have	or	by
one	Free Space	had
not	be	this

cut along the heavier solid line

Scholastic Professional Books • Learning Sight Words Is Easy!

Sight-Word Bingo Cards #31-40

Directions: Reproduce, laminate, and cut each card.

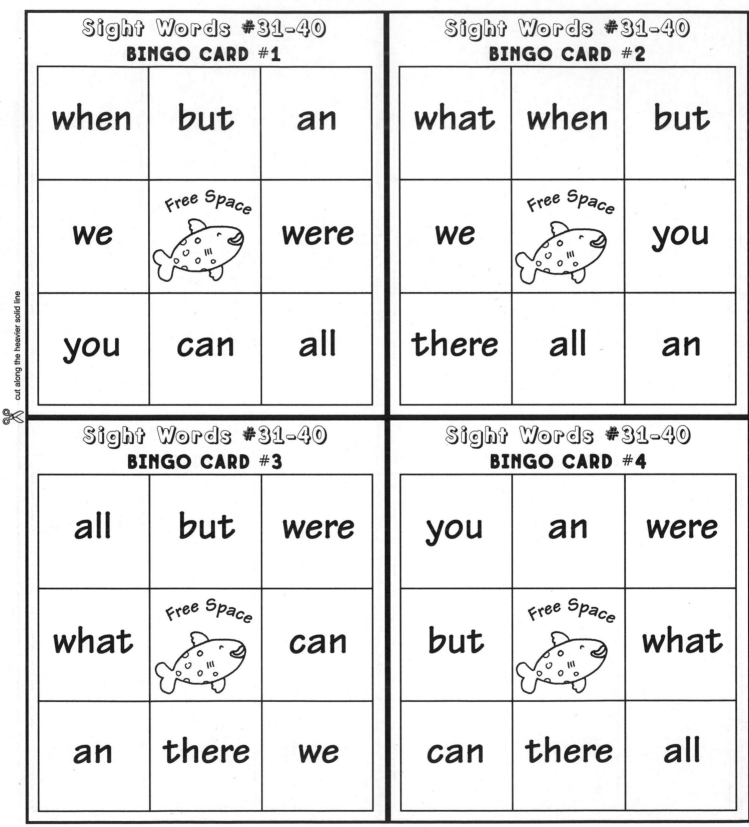

Sight Words #31-40
BINGO CARD #1

when	but	an
we	*Free Space*	were
you	can	all

Sight Words #31-40
BINGO CARD #2

what	when	but
we	*Free Space*	you
there	all	an

Sight Words #31-40
BINGO CARD #3

all	but	were
what	*Free Space*	can
an	there	we

Sight Words #31-40
BINGO CARD #4

you	an	were
but	*Free Space*	what
can	there	all

Sight-Word Bingo Cards #31-40

Directions: Reproduce, laminate, and cut each card.

Sight Words #31-40
BINGO CARD #5

but	what	all
were	Free Space	when
we	there	can

Sight Words #31-40
BINGO CARD #6

an	your	but
what	Free Space	all
were	when	we

Sight Words #31-40
BINGO CARD #7

there	can	an
your	Free Space	but
what	all	were

Sight Words #31-40
BINGO CARD #8

when	we	there
can	Free Space	an
your	but	what

Sight-Word Bingo Cards #41-50

Directions: Reproduce, laminate, and cut each card.

Sight Words #41-50
BINGO CARD #1

up	said	their
do	Free Space	will
about	when	each

Sight Words #41-50
BINGO CARD #2

said	do	up
will	Free Space	how
about	if	their

Sight Words #41-50
BINGO CARD #3

which	said	up
if	Free Space	how
each	their	will

Sight Words #41-50
BINGO CARD #4

each	up	which
if	Free Space	will
do	said	about

Sight-Word Bingo Cards #41-50

Directions: Reproduce, laminate, and cut each card.

Sight Words #41-50
BINGO CARD #5

which	their	said
if	Free Space	do
will	each	about

Sight Words #41-50
BINGO CARD #6

how	up	which
their	Free Space	said
if	do	will

Sight Words #41-50
BINGO CARD #7

each	about	how
up	Free Space	which
their	said	if

Sight Words #41-50
BINGO CARD #8

do	will	each
about	Free Space	how
up	which	their

Sight-Word Bingo Cards #51-60

Directions: Reproduce, laminate, and cut each card.

Sight Words #51-60
BINGO CARD #1

she	then	some
these	Free Space	other
would	them	so

Sight Words #51-60
BINGO CARD #2

then	out	them
so	Free Space	she
other	many	these

Sight Words #51-60
BINGO CARD #3

so	some	other
she	Free Space	out
many	these	would

Sight Words #51-60
BINGO CARD #4

out	then	would
some	Free Space	she
other	many	them

Sight-Word Bingo Cards #51-60

Directions: Reproduce, laminate, and cut each card.

Sight Words #51-60
BINGO CARD #5

out	them	then
she	Free Space	many
some	so	these

Sight Words #51-60
BINGO CARD #6

would	other	out
them	Free Space	then
she	many	some

Sight Words #51-60
BINGO CARD #7

so	these	would
other	Free Space	out
them	then	she

Sight Words #51-60
BINGO CARD #8

many	some	so
these	Free Space	would
other	out	them

Sight-Word Bingo Cards #61-70

Directions: Reproduce, laminate, and cut each card.

Sight Words #61-70
BINGO CARD #1

could	more	into
him	Free Space	two
has	like	time

Sight Words #61-70
BINGO CARD #2

see	has	could
into	Free Space	like
two	more	her

Sight Words #61-70
BINGO CARD #3

her	into	time
more	Free Space	like
him	see	could

Sight Words #61-70
BINGO CARD #4

has	him	see
could	Free Space	two
time	her	like

Sight-Word Bingo Cards #61-70

Directions: Reproduce, laminate, and cut each card.

Sight Words #61-70
BINGO CARD #5

into	has	more
her	*Free Space*	two
like	him	see

Sight Words #61-70
BINGO CARD #6

him	see	time
could	*Free Space*	into
has	more	her

Sight Words #61-70
BINGO CARD #7

time	could	into
has	*Free Space*	more
her	two	like

Sight Words #61-70
BINGO CARD #8

two	like	him
see	*Free Space*	time
could	into	has

Sight-Word Bingo Cards #71-80
Directions: Reproduce, laminate, and cut each card.

Sight Words #71-80
BINGO CARD #1

its	first	people
than	Free Space BICYCLE	now
been	no	my

Sight Words #71-80
BINGO CARD #2

no	people	been
first	Free Space BICYCLE	than
my	who	make

Sight Words #71-80
BINGO CARD #3

make	been	my
people	Free Space BICYCLE	first
who	now	than

Sight Words #71-80
BINGO CARD #4

now	its	people
than	Free Space BICYCLE	who
make	my	first

Sight-Word Bingo Cards #71-80

Directions: Reproduce, laminate, and cut each card.

Sight Words #71-80
BINGO CARD #5

no	make	than
first	Free Space	been
its	who	now

Sight Words #71-80
BINGO CARD #6

people	my	no
make	Free Space	than
first	been	its

Sight Words #71-80
BINGO CARD #7

who	now	people
my	Free Space	no
make	than	first

Sight Words #71-80
BINGO CARD #8

been	its	who
now	Free Space	people
my	no	make

cut along the heavier solid line

Scholastic Professional Books • Learning Sight Words Is Easy!

Sight-Word Bingo Cards #81-90

Directions: Reproduce, laminate, and cut each card.

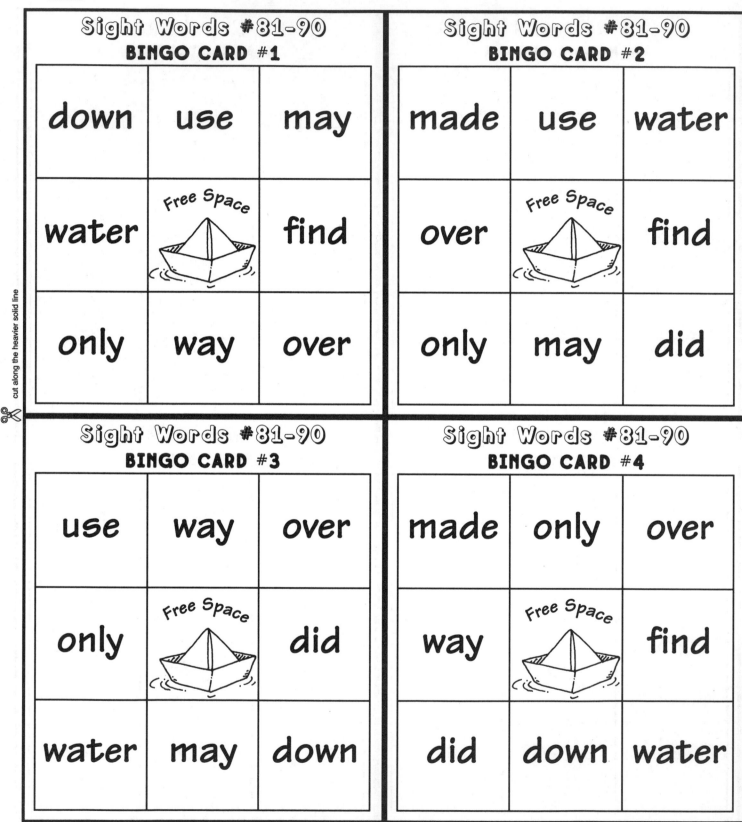

Sight Words #81-90
BINGO CARD #1

down	use	may
water	Free Space	find
only	way	over

Sight Words #81-90
BINGO CARD #2

made	use	water
over	Free Space	find
only	may	did

Sight Words #81-90
BINGO CARD #3

use	way	over
only	Free Space	did
water	may	down

Sight Words #81-90
BINGO CARD #4

made	only	over
way	Free Space	find
did	down	water

Sight-Word Bingo Cards #81-90

Directions: Reproduce, laminate, and cut each card.

Sight Words #81-90
BINGO CARD #5

made	over	did
down	Free Space	only
way	find	use

Sight Words #81-90
BINGO CARD #6

may	water	made
over	Free Space	did
down	only	way

Sight Words #81-90
BINGO CARD #7

find	use	may
water	Free Space	made
over	did	down

Sight Words #81-90
BINGO CARD #8

only	way	find
use	Free Space	may
water	made	over

Sight-Word Bingo Cards #91-100

Directions: Reproduce, laminate, and cut each card.

Sight Words #91-100
BINGO CARD #1

little	called	most
know	Free Space	just
where	after	very

Sight Words #91-100
BINGO CARD #2

after	words	little
just	Free Space	very
most	called	long

Sight Words #91-100
BINGO CARD #3

little	after	where
words	Free Space	long
most	just	know

Sight Words #91-100
BINGO CARD #4

know	just	where
called	Free Space	little
long	very	words

Sight-Word Bingo Cards #91-100

Directions: Reproduce, laminate, and cut each card.

Sight Words #91-100
BINGO CARD #5

long	little	very
after	Free Space	words
called	just	where

Sight Words #91-100
BINGO CARD #6

most	know	long
little	Free Space	very
after	words	called

Sight Words #91-100
BINGO CARD #7

just	where	most
know	Free Space	long
little	very	after

Sight Words #91-100
BINGO CARD #8

words	called	just
where	Free Space	must
know	long	little

Sight Word Bingo Cards (blank)

Directions: Reproduce, laminate, and cut each card.

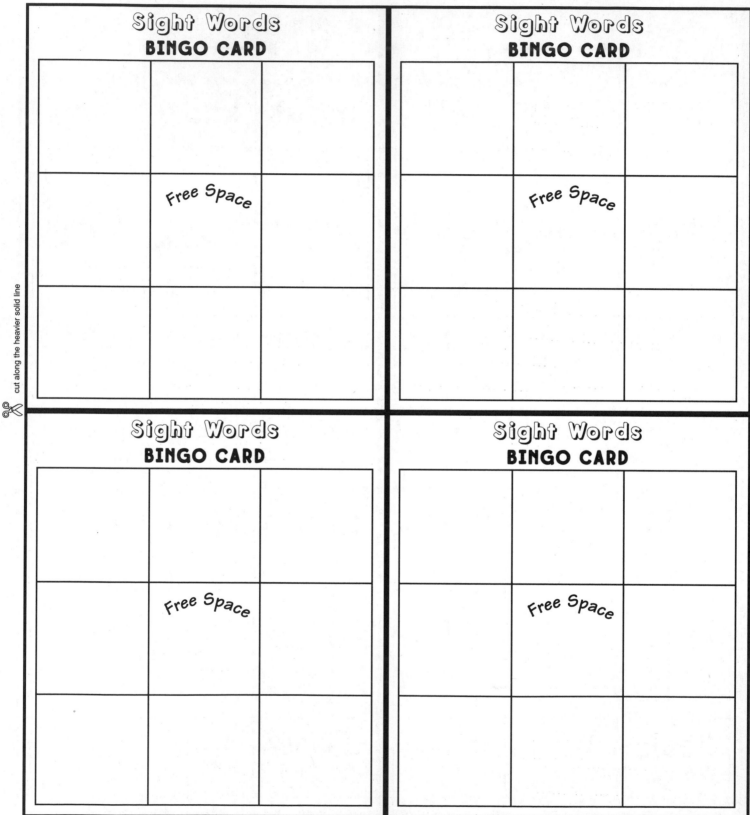

Word-Search Puzzle #1-10

Directions: Find each of the sight words hidden in the word search. Words appear across or down. Use a crayon to color in each word.

the	of	and	a	to
in	is	you	that	it

D	L	S	Z	U	Q	Q	Y	R	H	O	H
O	Y	O	U	S	G	O	M	Y	R	T	Q
L	U	T	Z	F	Q	X	P	X	N	M	L
X	Y	T	P	E	G	F	S	Y	Q	B	Q
A	O	O	L	B	Z	D	P	B	E	R	I
I	Q	K	L	F	R	E	M	N	U	L	T
D	I	Z	J	D	O	F	V	T	X	Q	Q
N	T	T	Y	M	J	C	X	V	L	C	W
T	I	S	B	K	Y	B	E	F	D	P	D
Q	P	R	T	A	N	D	X	T	H	A	T
I	N	R	H	V	J	Z	U	F	E	K	E
P	F	Y	Z	J	T	H	E	H	D	F	Z

Name: _____

Word-Search Puzzle #11-20

Directions: Find each of the sight words hidden in the word search. Words appear across or down. Use a crayon to color in each word.

he	for	was	on	are
as	with	his	they	at

J	O	R	W	Y	Y	C	D	O	U	X	B
A	T	W	V	K	O	R	L	H	Y	Z	S
P	H	D	F	P	M	J	F	M	R	Y	R
Z	G	O	N	N	G	X	M	I	N	O	I
J	E	H	F	X	T	U	Q	R	H	T	B
S	W	T	H	E	Y	I	B	M	A	V	Q
H	E	O	P	O	H	I	S	U	Q	S	T
W	E	L	U	A	L	B	N	H	B	C	G
N	Q	B	J	Y	W	W	A	S	I	G	H
B	Z	E	F	O	R	B	F	H	A	S	U
Q	C	G	D	F	O	E	Q	C	L	T	I
W	I	T	H	B	H	A	R	E	S	W	O

Scholastic Professional Books • Learning Sight Words Is Easy!

Word-Search Puzzle #21-30

Directions: Find each of the sight words hidden in the word search. Words appear across or down. Use a crayon to color in each word.

be	this	from	I	have
or	by	one	had	not

S	R	Q	B	P	Y	Z	H	E	J	H	Y
H	A	V	E	G	G	Q	T	P	H	S	I
S	A	S	Q	D	S	J	N	W	P	M	A
R	O	J	H	A	D	O	T	A	A	O	T
H	U	V	S	H	O	K	C	K	C	R	E
R	R	T	O	N	E	X	T	O	G	C	G
T	Z	M	F	U	P	J	M	Z	J	Y	F
T	H	I	S	Q	O	D	Y	L	Q	B	R
T	C	Q	F	G	T	Z	T	X	O	X	W
Q	P	S	F	R	O	M	T	D	T	D	K
P	S	V	X	B	K	P	M	L	N	O	T
Z	R	T	D	Y	P	B	E	Z	P	J	T

Name: _____

Word-Search Puzzle
#31-40

Directions: Find each of the sight words hidden in the word search. Words appear across or down. Use a crayon to color in each word.

but	what	all	were	when
we	there	can	an	your

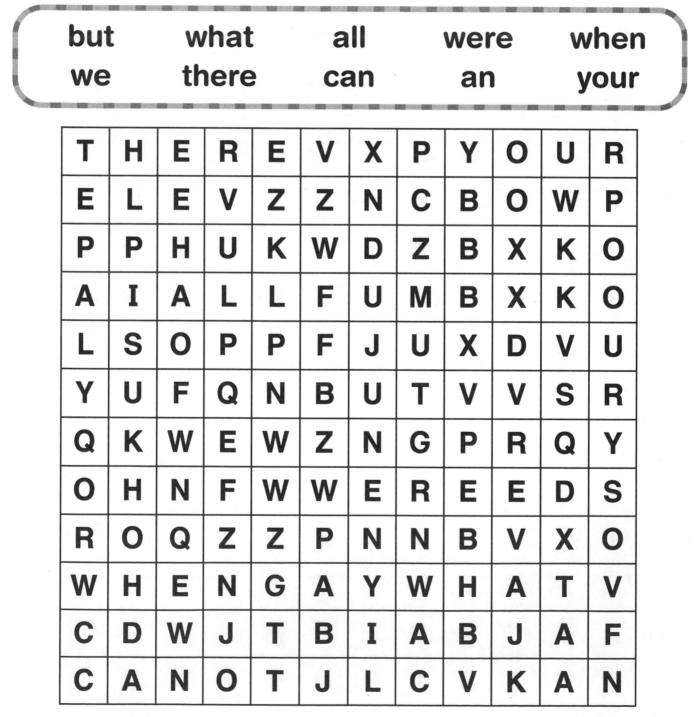

T	H	E	R	E	V	X	P	Y	O	U	R
E	L	E	V	Z	Z	N	C	B	O	W	P
P	P	H	U	K	W	D	Z	B	X	K	O
A	I	A	L	L	F	U	M	B	X	K	O
L	S	O	P	P	F	J	U	X	D	V	U
Y	U	F	Q	N	B	U	T	V	V	S	R
Q	K	W	E	W	Z	N	G	P	R	Q	Y
O	H	N	F	W	W	E	R	E	E	D	S
R	O	Q	Z	Z	P	N	N	B	V	X	O
W	H	E	N	G	A	Y	W	H	A	T	V
C	D	W	J	T	B	I	A	B	J	A	F
C	A	N	O	T	J	L	C	V	K	A	N

Name: _____

Word-Search Puzzle
#41-50

Directions: Find each of the sight words hidden in the word search. Words appear across or down. Use a crayon to color in each word.

| which | | their | | said | | if | | do |
| will | | each | | about | | how | | up |

S	A	I	D	C	Y	Z	E	V	B	U	D
V	D	O	Z	B	A	F	Q	S	R	K	T
U	K	I	N	A	B	O	U	T	R	D	P
X	G	V	O	V	O	E	L	W	R	S	E
Q	N	J	Q	T	Y	X	L	T	U	J	J
W	I	L	L	U	H	O	W	A	D	I	I
I	R	X	S	M	J	V	B	U	Z	S	B
I	F	H	R	Z	F	J	B	G	F	L	Y
N	S	F	U	P	O	K	T	B	U	Z	O
W	H	I	C	H	J	C	O	R	N	S	O
I	K	E	B	E	H	C	E	A	C	H	R
T	H	E	I	R	S	Q	Q	V	A	U	R

71

Word-Search Puzzle #51-60

Directions: Find each of the sight words hidden in the word search. Words appear across or down. Use a crayon to color in each word.

out	them	then	she	many
some	so	these	would	other

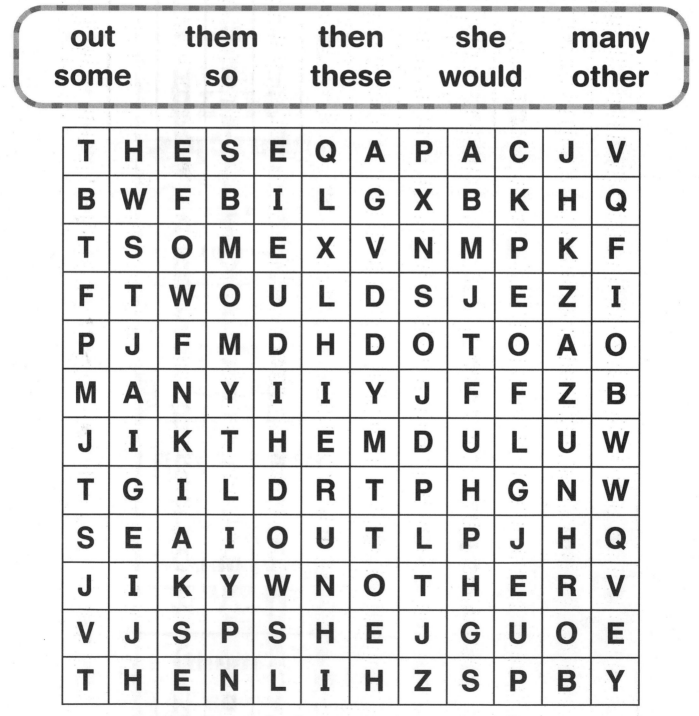

T	H	E	S	E	Q	A	P	A	C	J	V
B	W	F	B	I	L	G	X	B	K	H	Q
T	S	O	M	E	X	V	N	M	P	K	F
F	T	W	O	U	L	D	S	J	E	Z	I
P	J	F	M	D	H	D	O	T	O	A	O
M	A	N	Y	I	I	Y	J	F	F	Z	B
J	I	K	T	H	E	M	D	U	L	U	W
T	G	I	L	D	R	T	P	H	G	N	W
S	E	A	I	O	U	T	L	P	J	H	Q
J	I	K	Y	W	N	O	T	H	E	R	V
V	J	S	P	S	H	E	J	G	U	O	E
T	H	E	N	L	I	H	Z	S	P	B	Y

Scholastic Professional Books • *Learning Sight Words Is Easy!*

Word-Search Puzzle
#61-70

Directions: Find each of the sight words hidden in the word search. Words appear across or down. Use a crayon to color in each word.

into	has	more	her	two
like	him	see	time	could

C	O	U	L	D	Q	T	R	T	X	M	O
O	K	W	M	F	Z	R	U	O	Q	B	W
H	I	M	S	W	D	D	S	A	L	P	J
L	M	H	S	E	E	B	B	Y	I	E	T
W	M	E	E	O	Q	Z	S	D	V	C	C
R	S	H	W	I	N	T	O	E	V	V	F
W	T	Q	M	A	A	P	A	K	Q	L	K
V	O	N	V	F	V	H	A	S	W	P	Y
H	Z	P	M	O	R	E	P	E	Q	C	E
H	E	R	O	Y	S	P	L	I	K	E	A
H	U	F	M	G	Z	X	M	J	T	W	O
T	I	M	E	T	A	B	D	Z	K	M	R

Word-Search Puzzle #71-80

Directions: Find each of the sight words hidden in the word search. Words appear across or down. Use a crayon to color in each word.

no	make	than	first	been
its	who	now	people	my

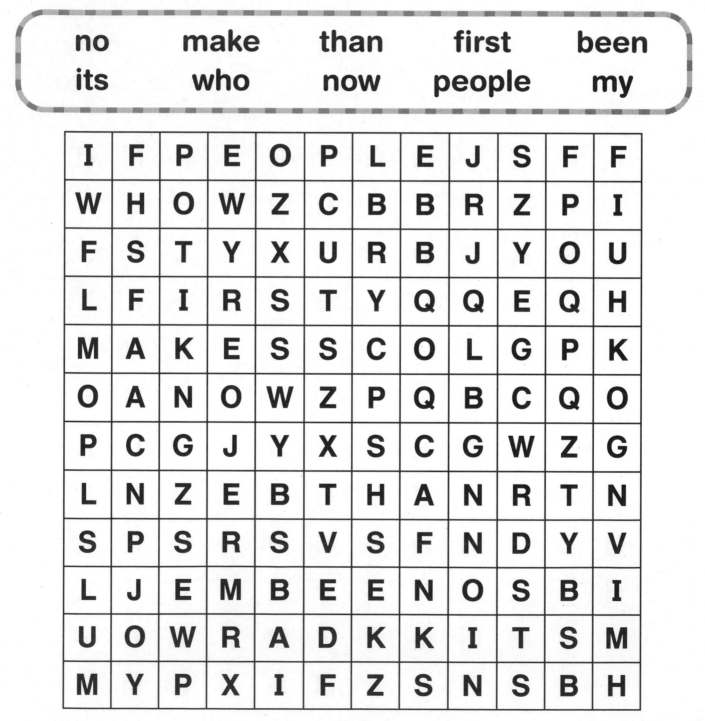

I	F	P	E	O	P	L	E	J	S	F	F
W	H	O	W	Z	C	B	B	R	Z	P	I
F	S	T	Y	X	U	R	B	J	Y	O	U
L	F	I	R	S	T	Y	Q	Q	E	Q	H
M	A	K	E	S	S	C	O	L	G	P	K
O	A	N	O	W	Z	P	Q	B	C	Q	O
P	C	G	J	Y	X	S	C	G	W	Z	G
L	N	Z	E	B	T	H	A	N	R	T	N
S	P	S	R	S	V	S	F	N	D	Y	V
L	J	E	M	B	E	E	N	O	S	B	I
U	O	W	R	A	D	K	K	I	T	S	M
M	Y	P	X	I	F	Z	S	N	S	B	H

Scholastic Professional Books • *Learning Sight Words Is Easy!*

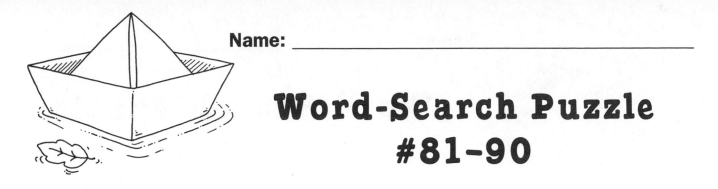

Name: _____

Word-Search Puzzle #81-90

Directions: Find each of the sight words hidden in the word search. Words appear across or down. Use a crayon to color in each word.

made	over	did	down	only
way	find	use	may	water

L	C	H	E	W	A	Y	C	Z	B	K	Z
D	I	D	N	Y	C	D	U	P	I	C	M
D	R	A	G	P	M	R	O	L	Y	W	O
F	I	N	D	B	G	M	S	F	W	N	U
A	Q	B	U	V	N	C	D	P	J	N	Y
D	X	O	V	E	R	W	X	P	X	Q	R
U	E	U	W	N	J	U	G	F	W	U	S
H	B	N	J	U	S	E	C	I	M	N	P
Q	D	O	W	N	O	M	P	H	Q	P	X
E	S	T	B	H	G	C	Z	G	B	U	L
U	G	W	A	T	E	R	B	F	M	A	Y
O	N	L	Y	L	E	M	A	D	E	S	K

Word-Search Puzzle #91-100

Directions: Find each of the sight words hidden in the word search. Words appear across or down. Use a crayon to color in each word.

long	little	very	after	words
called	just	where	most	know

O	Y	Y	Z	Q	J	T	A	F	T	E	R
L	O	N	G	R	T	W	V	F	G	P	Y
J	U	S	T	X	C	A	F	V	G	P	H
Z	B	L	G	O	T	D	X	Y	P	B	E
D	N	F	G	U	K	R	Y	D	J	Q	L
T	F	W	C	W	O	R	D	S	L	S	X
P	Y	Q	C	T	M	M	O	S	T	B	B
K	N	O	W	O	X	M	Z	R	Z	T	T
F	U	W	R	K	E	Z	W	H	E	R	E
C	A	L	L	E	D	J	N	T	X	C	R
B	Q	I	I	M	Y	L	I	T	T	L	E
V	E	R	Y	X	U	T	K	O	H	F	P

Scholastic Professional Books • Learning Sight Words Is Easy!

Fun Flash Cards
#1-10

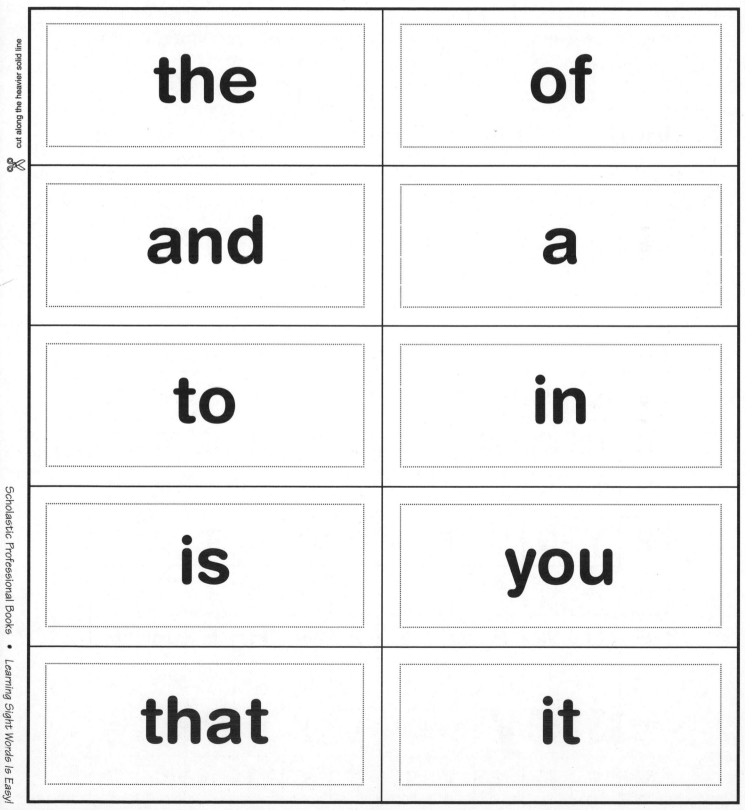

the	of
and	a
to	in
is	you
that	it

Fun Flash Cards
#11-20

he	for
was	on
are	as
with	his
they	at

Scholastic Professional Books • *Learning Sight Words Is Easy!*

Fun Flash Cards
#21-30

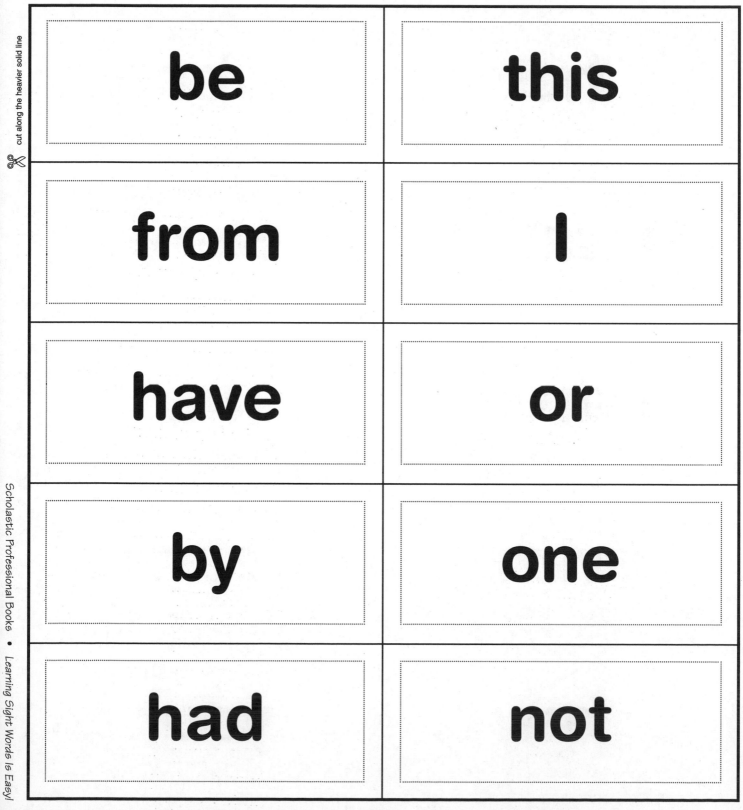

be	this
from	I
have	or
by	one
had	not

Scholastic Professional Books • Learning Sight Words Is Easy!

Fun Flash Cards
#31–40

cut along the heavier solid line

but	what
all	were
when	we
there	can
an	your

Scholastic Professional Books • Learning Sight Words Is Easy!

Fun Flash Cards
#41-50

which	their
said	if
do	will
each	about
how	up

Scholastic Professional Books • Learning Sight Words Is Easy!

cut along the heavier solid line

out	them
then	she
many	some
so	these
would	other

Scholastic Professional Books • *Learning Sight Words Is Easy!*

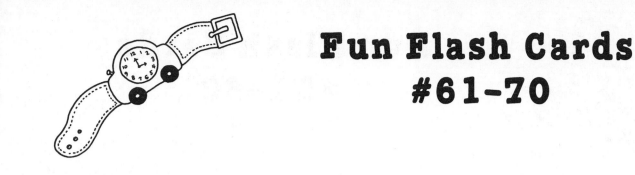

Fun Flash Cards
#61-70

into	has
more	her
two	like
him	see
time	could

Fun Flash Cards
#71-80

no	make
than	first
been	its
who	now
people	my

Scholastic Professional Books • Learning Sight Words Is Easy!

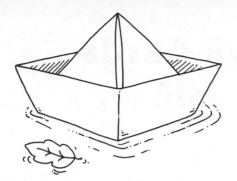

cut along the heavier solid line

Scholastic Professional Books • Learning Sight Words Is Easy!

made	**over**
did	**down**
only	**way**
find	**use**
may	**water**

Fun Flash Cards
#91-100

long	little
very	after
words	called
just	where
most	know

Scholastic Professional Books • Learning Sight Words Is Easy!

Fun Flash Cards
(blank)

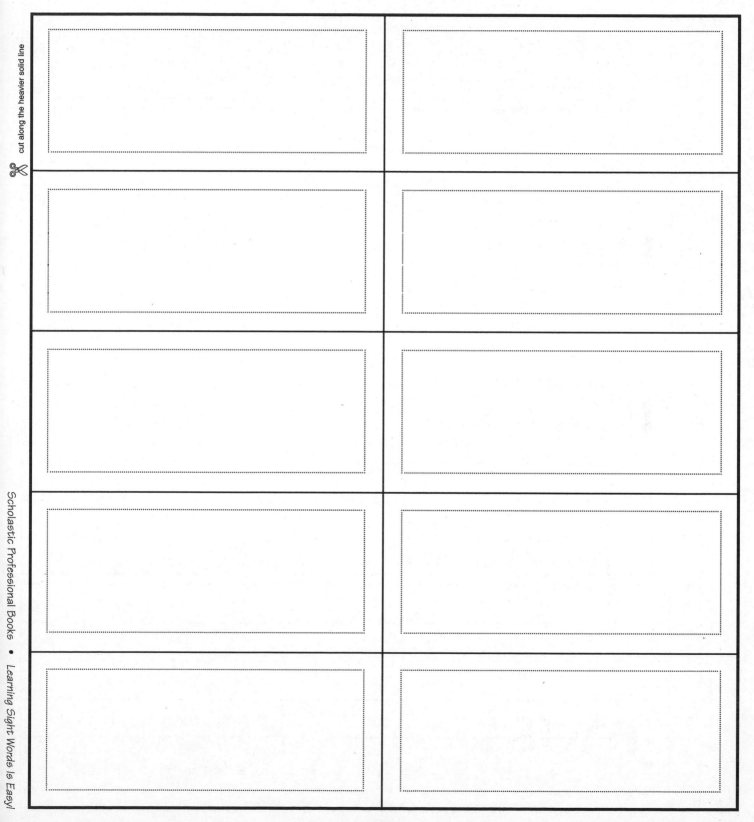

Scholastic Professional Books • Learning Sight Words Is Easy!

Strategic Assessment Tool

Student: _____ Grade: _____ Teacher: _____ Year: _____

Sight Word	Baseline Date	Date	Date	Date	Date
1. the					
2. of					
3. and					
4. a					
5. to					
6. in					
7. is					
8. you					
9. that					
10. it					
11. he					
12. for					
13. was					
14. on					
15. are					
16. as					
17. with					
18. his					
19. they					
20. at					
21. be					
22. this					
23. from					
24. I					
25. have					
SCORE	/25	/25	/25	/25	/25

Sight Word	Baseline Date	Date	Date	Date	Date
26. or					
27. by					
28. one					
29. had					
30. not					
31. but					
32. what					
33. all					
34. were					
35. when					
36. we					
37. there					
38. can					
39. an					
40. your					
41. which					
42. their					
43. said					
44. if					
45. do					
46. will					
47. each					
48. about					
49. how					
50. up					
SCORE	/25	/25	/25	/25	/25

Sight Word	Baseline Date	Date	Date	Date	Date
51. out					
52. them					
53. then					
54. she					
55. many					
56. some					
57. so					
58. these					
59. would					
60. other					
61. into					
62. has					
63. more					
64. her					
65. two					
66. like					
67. him					
68. see					
69. time					
70. could					
71. no					
72. make					
73. than					
74. first					
75. been					
SCORE	/25	/25	/25	/25	/25

Sight Word	Baseline Date	Date	Date	Date	Date
76. its					
77. who					
78. now					
79. people					
80. my					
81. made					
82. over					
83. did					
84. down					
85. only					
86. way					
87. find					
88. use					
89. may					
90. water					
91. long					
92. little					
93. very					
94. after					
95. words					
96. called					
97. just					
98. where					
99. most					
100. know					
SCORE	/25	/25	/25	/25	/25
TOTAL SCORE	/100	/100	/100	/100	/100

Scholastic Professional Books • Learning Sight Words Is Easy!

Dear Family,

   Please support classroom learning by practicing the attached Read & Spell Flash Cards with your child. Since sight words appear most frequently in the writing children encounter, learning them is key to your child's success as a reader.

   Have your child cut apart the flash cards and store them in a sealed bag. Encourage her/him to review the flash cards often. In order to reinforce how to spell the words, have your child read the word, then turn the card over and write the word from memory. Work together, checking to see if the spelling is correct. If the "R" is circled on the flash card, your child needs to learn how to read the word. If the "S" is circled, your child needs to learn how to spell the word.

   Thank you for your support.

Name: _____

Read & Spell Flash Cards

Directions: If the "R" is circled on the flash card, you need to review how to read the word. If the "S" is circled, you need to review how to spell the word. Cut apart the Read & Spell Flash Cards and store them in a sealed bag. You will need to review the flash cards often.

- **Read the word.**
- **Turn the card over and write the word.**
- **Check to see if the spelling is correct.**

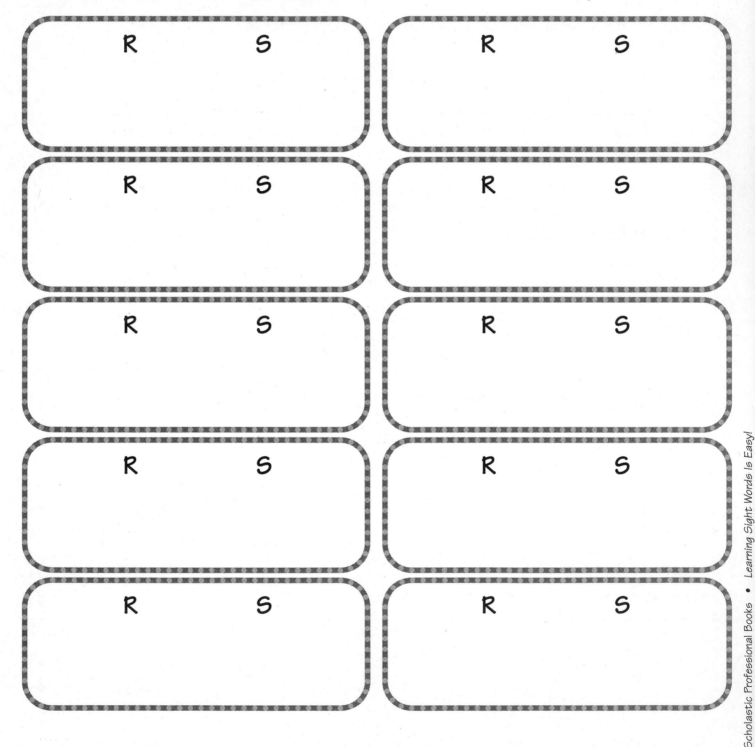

Celebrate Achievement

To keep students engaged in the process of learning sight words, reward effort and achievement. If you like, use the ideas below to help make learning sight words a fun endeavor.

Try these fun ideas!

First 100 Words Party: As soon as the class has cumulatively mastered 100 words, have a party. When they master another 100 words, have another party!

BINGO Fest: Eat cupcakes! Drink juice! And play sight-word BINGO!

Sight-Word-of-the-Day: Write the word on a corner of your chalkboard. Ask students to look for the word as they do shared reading. As soon as children spot a sight word, they must raise their hands briefly. When every child has spotted at least one sight word it's time to celebrate. Invite the children to raise their hands above their heads and shout, "Hip Hip Hooray! We Read Sight Words Today!" You may also use this fun activity as a diagnostic tool. Some children may recognize sight words but cannot yet read them, so look to see which hands go up.

Certificates of Achievement: After each child learns yet another ten sight words, provide him/her with a certificate. Promote student self-confidence and literacy!

How to Use Sight-Word Certificates

By inviting students to decorate their very own certificates, you provide them with an opportunity to recognize and internalize their growing abilities.

- Supply students with copies of the certificate on page 92.
- Ask students to write the sight words they can spell on the certificate.
- Invite students to decorate certificates with markers, glued-on glitter, and stickers.
- Students may share the completed certificates with each other and family members.

Certificate of Achievement

is presented to

Look at all the sight words you learned to read and spell.
You're on the path to literacy. Congratulations!

Teacher

Date

was

they

is

when

we

said

an

will

said

an

that

in

you

to

Word-Search Answer Key

Word Search #1-10

```
D L S Z U Q Q Y R H O H
O Y O U S G O M Y R T Q
L U T Z F Q X P X N M L
X Y T P E G F S Y Q B Q
A O O L B Z D P B E R I
I Q K L F R E M N U L T
D I Z J D O F V T X Q Q
N T T Y M J C X V L C W
T I S B K Y B E F D P D
Q P R T A N D X T H A T
I N R H V J Z U F E K E
P F Y Z J T H E H D F Z
```

Word Search #11-20

```
J O R W Y Y C D O U X B
A T W V K O R L H Y Z S
P H D F P M J F M R Y R
Z G O N G X M I N O I
J E H F X T U Q R H T B
S W T H E Y I B M A V Q
H E O P O H I S U Q S T
W E L U A L B N H B C G
N Q B J Y W W A S I G H
B Z E F O R B F H A S U
Q C G D F O E Q C L T I
W I T H B H A R E S W O
```

Word Search #21-30

```
S R Q B P Y Z H E J H Y
H A V E G G Q T P H S I
S A S Q D S J N W P M A
R O J H A D O T A A O T
H U V S H O K C K C R E
R R T O N E X T O G C G
T Z M F U P J M Z J Y F
T H I S Q O D Y L Q B R
T C Q F G T Z T X O X W
Q P S F R O M T D T D K
P S V X B K P M L N O T
Z R T D Y P B E Z P J T
```

Word Search #31-40

```
T H E R E V X P Y O U R
E L E V Z Z N C B O W P
P P H U K W D Z B X K O
A I A L L F U M B X K O
L S O P P F J U X D V U
Y U F Q N B U T V V S R
Q K W E W Z N G P R Q Y
O H N F W W E R E E D S
R O Q Z Z P N N B V X O
W H E N G A Y W H A T V
C D W J T B I A B J A F
C A N O T J L C V K A N
```

Word Search #41-50

```
S A I D C Y Z E V B U D
V D O Z B A F Q S R K T
U K I N A B O U T R D P
X G V O V O E L W R S E
Q N J Q T Y X L T U J J
W I L L U H O W A D I I
I R X S M J V B U Z S B
I F H R Z F J B G F L Y
N S F U P O K T B U Z O
W H I C H J C O R N S O
I K E B E H C E A C H R
T H E I R S Q Q V A U R
```

Word Search #51-60

```
T H E S E Q A P A C J V
B W F B I L G X B K H Q
T S O M E X V N M P K F
F T W O U L D S J E Z I
P J F M D H D O T O A O
M A N Y I I Y J F F Z B
J I K T H E M D U L U W
T G I L D R T P H G N W
S E A I O U T L P J H Q
J I K Y W N O T H E R V
V J S P S H E J G U O E
T H E N L I H Z S P B Y
```

Word Search #61-70

```
C O U L D Q T R T X M O
O K W M F Z R U O Q B W
H I M S W D D S A L P J
L M H S E E B B Y I E T
W M E E O Q Z S D V C C
R S H W I N T O E V V F
W T Q M A A P A K Q L K
V O N V F V H A S W P Y
H Z P M O R E P E Q C E
H E R O Y S P L I K E A
H U F M G Z X M J T W O
T I M E T A B D Z K M R
```

Word Search #71-80

```
I F P E O P L E J S F F
W H O W Z C B B R Z P I
F S T Y X U R B J Y O U
L F I R S T Y Q Q E Q H
M A K E S S C O L G P K
O A N O W Z P Q B C Q O
P C G J Y X S C G W Z G
L N Z E B T H A N R T N
S P S R S V S F N D Y V
L J E M B E E N O S B I
U O W R A D K K I T S M
M Y P X I F Z S N S B H
```

Word Search #81-90

```
L C H E W A Y C Z B K Z
D I D N Y C D U P I C M
D R A G P M R O L Y W O
F I N D B G M S F W N U
A Q B U V N C D P J N Y
D X O V E R W X P X Q R
U E U W N J U G F W U S
H B N J U S E C I M N P
Q D O W N O M P H Q P X
E S T B H G C Z G B U L
U G W A T E R B F M A Y
O N L Y L E M A D E S K
```

Word Search #91-100

```
O Y Y Z Q J T A F T E R
L O N G R T W V F G P Y
J U S T X C A F V G P H
Z B L G O T D X Y P B E
D N F G U K R Y D J Q L
T F W C W O R D S L S X
P Y Q C T M M O S T B B
K N O W O X M Z R Z T T
F U W R K E Z W H E R E
C A L L E D J N T X C R
B Q I I M Y L I T T L E
V E R Y X U T K O H F P
```

93

Notes

Notes

Notes